For by
FAITH

JESSE DUPLANTIS

Harrison House

Tulsa, OK

This book is dedicated to my precious Covenant Partners around the world. Together, we are reaching people and changing lives, one soul at a time!

18 17 16 15 14   7 6 5 4 3 2 1

For by IT...FAITH
ISBN: 978-160683-986-7
Copyright © 2014 Jesse Duplantis

Published in Partnership with:
Jesse Duplantis Ministries
P.O. Box 1089
Destrehan, LA 70047
www.jdm.org

Harrison House Publishers
Tulsa, OK 74145
www.harrisonhouse.com

Jesse Duplantis Ministries is dedicated to reaching people and changing lives with the Gospel of Jesus Christ. For more information or to purchase other products from Jesse Duplantis Ministries, please contact us at the address above.

Table of Contents

Chapter 1 For by IT... FAITH!..1

Chapter 2 FAITH Fuels Your Future.............................13

Chapter 3 Always TRIUMPH in Christ!....................23

Chapter 4 Be a "For by IT" Believer:
Live by the Faith of Jesus!.........................31

Chapter 5 Looking Unto JESUS...
The Author and Finisher of Our FAITH.........39

Chapter 6 Faith is More than Believing—It's DOING.........49

Chapter 7 Your FREEDOM Starts with a Choice—Make It!.......57

Chapter 8 Don't Give Up on Your Faith.................65

Chapter 9 It's a Question of Faith
"Do you believe that I am able to do this?" – Jesus 71

Chapter 10 Refuse to Shipwreck Your Own Faith.................81

*Now **faith** is the substance of things hoped for,*
the evidence of things not seen.
***For by it** the elders obtained a good report.*

Hebrews 11:1-2

If You Don't Know What "IT" is,
You Won't Have It!

For by
FAITH

For by IT...FA<u>IT</u>H!

O ne of the things I love the most about my life is the relationship that I've developed with God over the years. He is my Father and I am one of His sons—and I love putting my faith in Him and being in His family. Glory!

As I was reading His Word the other day, He brought me to a familiar passage of scripture—and a portion of that scripture jumped off the page at me in a way I had never thought about before. It blessed me so much that I knew I had to share it with you! Go with me now to the book of Hebrews 11:1-2...

> *"Now faith is the substance of things hoped for, the evidence of things not seen. <u>For by it</u> the elders obtained a good report."*

Faith! "For by IT"
All Good and Perfect Things Exist

"For by it"—those three little words struck my spirit and God began to reveal some things to me. Think about this for a minute: If it wasn't for faith, "relationship" wouldn't exist, "hope" wouldn't exist, and "love" wouldn't exist either. In fact, if it wasn't for faith,

nothing of true value would exist at all.

"For by it"—those words are burning inside me. Without faith, you not only cannot please God, but you also cannot enjoy the Spirit of God or produce the fruit of His Spirit in your life. The same is true with everything that is of true value. *Every* good and perfect gift comes from above—but you can't access any of them unless you have faith in the One handing out these good and perfect gifts. Faith is required to access truth, salvation, real wisdom and understanding, and every other good thing that exists.

Without faith, nothing that your soul needs or desires can *exist* for you…nothing. *"The elders"* of faith mentioned in Hebrews 11:1-2 understood this and that's how they *"obtained a good report."* Who was making this report? God Himself! You cannot get what you really need on your own. We all want to be happy, and yet not one of us can be truly happy without an abiding connection to the Father. This is why salvation is the first step towards "the good life." And, guess what? That, too, requires faith! *"For by it"* you look to God. *"For by it"* you recognize that not only does God exist, but that He also loves you—and you need Him to be happy.

Faith! "For by IT"
You Gain "The Blessing" of Riches with no Added Sorrow

Many people think that if they could only be rich, they'd be happy. Before I was saved, I thought that way, too. I found out I was wrong. I worked and became successful—I could buy anything

I wanted, but I still wasn't happy. In fact, I remember being so disappointed that money itself didn't give me what I really wanted, which was happiness.

There's nothing wrong with money. God lives in a place with gold streets! There is no lack in Heaven. But you were never created to put something as powerful as your *faith* in something as temporal as money. *"For what is a man profited, if he shall gain the whole world, and lose his own soul?"* (Matthew 16:26). Your faith should be in God first—then you can gain the whole world *and* keep your soul. In other words, your mind, will, and emotions can grow rich, too.

Can you get rich without faith? Yes! Of course! But will it be *profitable* for you? No! Of course not! Without the "blessing of the Lord," you are in dire poverty no matter how much money you have.

If you want to really profit financially, focus on *faith*. It is better to be "blessed" than "rich"…but why choose when the scripture says you can have both? And with no sorrow either! *"The blessing of the Lord, it maketh rich, and He addeth no sorrow with it"* (Proverbs 10:22).

As believers, we need to put our faith in God so that we can access everything that is profitable—spiritually, physically, and financially. *"For by it"*—our faith in God—are we able to enjoy *"the blessing of the Lord"* that will not only *"maketh rich"* in every area of life, but with *"no sorrow"* added. That's a good life!

3

Faith! "For by IT"
You Find a Greater Desire for Integrity

Faith in God changes everything. One of the ways it changes you is by making you much more interested in doing what you *say*. When God's Word becomes more valuable to you, suddenly your word becomes more valuable to you, too. **Faith in the heart is closely connected with integrity in life.**

I told God years ago when I started this ministry that I would not fail Him in my service to Him—I would work. I also vowed to God that I would not fail the partners He sent to help me preach this Gospel—I would not fail them through scandals and such. Today, after 36 years in full-time ministry, I am very proud to say I have kept my promise both to God and to the partners He's sent to me.

How was I able to keep those vows to God? Three words: *"For by it."* My faith in God sustains me daily so that I can actually DO what I promise to do. Without faith, my strength and ability wavers. But, with faith, I am able to do ALL things…even hard things, day after day.

All you need is faith for today. Tomorrow has enough trouble of its own. Personally, I have created a habit of hearing the Word every day. I do this because I need faith every day. Why? So I can handle what comes up every day and fulfill my promises to God and to both my physical and spiritual family. Being a person of integrity isn't hard. Remember that all you need to concentrate on is developing faith *today*.

Faith! "For by IT"
Your Life Changes...and People Notice

Another thing faith does is make your life a living testament to God's power. You see, I've learned that people see more than they hear—and they notice when your faith in God becomes the center-point in your life. They may not understand your faith, but they most certainly see your works.

I've decided that if *"faith cometh by hearing, and hearing by the Word of God"* (Romans 10:17), then the more of the Word that I hear, the more I will be affected by what I hear...and the more I will act upon it and see change in my life.

Your faith will give shape and force to your actions. And people will SEE the shape and force of what you DO. So, if you don't like what you see in your own life today, change it! You can change things by using Romans 4:17 and calling those things in your life that are "NOT" as though they "WERE." Notice that the Word tells you to talk about it like it is in the past—as if it not only *will* happen, but has already *happened*. Abraham is called the father of faith because he did this very thing. Abraham called himself what God called him—the father of many nations—and he did it years before he ever had a child and before others saw him as an earthly father.

You see, nobody has to see it but God and you. But you can take it to the bank that if you hold onto your faith and apply Romans 4:17, others will see it...and then they will say it! That's what natural people do. Faith is going against that natural mindset. Faith is doing what Abraham did and saying what God has promised. Say what you *want* and not what you *have*. *"For by it"*—faith—you will get what you hope for but don't yet see in life.

Faith! "For by IT"
You Defend Yourself Against the Devil

I love what the covering of faith does. No matter what the devil does, if you have faith, then you know that God is with you—and your faith becomes an arrow-deflector! ***"For by it"* you protect yourself from every arrow and bullet of the devil.** So, in essence, you destroy the works of the devil. Notice that the Word calls your faith a "shield"—that means protection!

I like to say that faith is the main thread of the fabric of God's clothes, because faith is woven into everything that has anything to do with God. As I mentioned earlier, you can't even get saved without faith!

If the Word calls faith a shield, then obviously somebody's fighting us and God thinks we need a form of protection. The "armor of God" mentioned in Ephesians 6:11-17 paints a good visual picture of what God wants us to wear and to hold—all for the purpose of being *"able to stand against the wiles of the devil"* (Ephesians 6:11). God warns us to put on the "whole" armor—because if we take any of it off or lay any of it down, then we are not fully clothed. So, we are not fully protected or able to stand without it.

Loins girded with truth, chest covered with righteousness, and feet covered with the preparation of the Gospel of peace—these three the Bible tells us to put *"on."* But, notice, we are not told to put "on" the Word or put "on" our faith in God. No, the Sword and the Shield? Those two we are told to *"take!"* In other words, we must pick these weapons up daily and DO something with them. Each is a weapon against the works of the devil—one to attack and one to defend.

Only salvation (a helmet) do we both "take" and put "on." I believe the "taking" part comes when we are born again. Believing in your heart and confessing with your mouth that Jesus is Lord is about reaching out to accept ("take") what Jesus died to give us on the cross. After you accept Jesus as Lord (receive and take Him into your life), your "helmet" is in your possession and it's yours.

But now what do you do with your salvation? You put it "on" every day! You wrap it around your head—remind yourself what the blood has done for you personally—and refuse to allow the devil to weight your mind or your body with something Christ paid the cost for getting rid of in your life.

Now read Isaiah 53:4-5 and notice what the blood did for you. Grief and sorrow? They are under the blood, so they have no place under the helmet or in your mind! Neither do the rest. Transgressions? Iniquity? Lack of peace? Sickness of the body or sickness of the soul (mind, will, or emotions)? They are all under the blood and have NO place in or on your mind or your body.

Putting on the "helmet" is personal. It's reminding yourself of what the blood of Jesus did for YOU personally—and it's casting off whatever accusations or torment the devil tries to use against your mind or your body to rob you of what Jesus has done for you. There's a reason why the helmet is on your head: You have to remind your mind!

If you want to stand up against the devil, wear the armor. Put it "on" and "take" it up—and do it daily if you want to stand and win.

Faith! "For by IT"
You Find the Will to do What is Right

You must never turn back or hesitate on the path of duty. Faith in God can give you the good will to do what's right. If God has put something on your heart to do or if you have vowed to do something for someone or for God and you're struggling with your will to do it, let me help you: Focus on your faith. *"For by it"* you will find the will not only to do what's right, but also to actually enjoy it. God can turn your "duty" into something you don't mind doing, and maybe even come to enjoy.

Faith! "For by IT"
We Win Souls and Live a Life Worth Living

Whatever God has put on your heart to do, you *can* do! As you build faith, God will infuse you with whatever you need to get the job done. As you put on His armor, you will be equipped to handle whatever comes each day…and enjoy your life, too!

You CAN stand up against the works of the devil and win! You CAN win souls and have a life that is worth living—full of joy, power, integrity, and all the multi-layered riches of being "blessed" by God. How will you do it? You'll do it with three little words: *"For by it."* You know, the Word tells us to "occupy until He comes" and I can't think of a better way to do that than to live by faith every day. How about you?

Always keep the faith. Keep it today, tomorrow, and the next day, too. If you make a habit out of it, I know that your life can be a good one. *"For by it"* you will see God's best in your life.

Chapter One Faith Declarations

Faith! *"For by it"* I access God and *everything* of true value. By FAITH, I receive every good and perfect gift from above. He's pleased with me—my report is GOOD!

Faith! *"For by it"* I gain the blessing of God and access everything that is *profitable.* By FAITH, all spiritual, physical and financial riches are mine—with no sorrow!

Faith! *"For by it"* I keep my vows to God and others. Day-by-day, my FAITH in God sustains me, inspires me, and propels me to do what's right!

Faith! *"For by it"* I defend myself! I put "on" and "take" the whole armor of God—truth, righteousness, the Gospel of peace, salvation, God's Word, and my FAITH!

Faith Testimony

I am so thankful for you and Cathy and your ministry. For years I was depressed and defeated and knew I needed to get myself in the company of some happy believers and to also learn to better encourage myself in the Lord.

Through Facebook, a relative of mine shared a link to your ministry. I clicked on it and watched you and God did a miraculous thing. Even though I've been a believer since I was twelve, I had become ungrateful and a habitual complainer. In the last several years, the Lord has been working with me to cast that off. Yet it wasn't until I watched you, that something broke loose and in the last month, I've become a real worshipper.

Every morning, my first thoughts when I wake up are of praise and gratitude and this continues with me all day long, and my last thoughts at night are of thankfulness and praise. My mom and I have begun praying daily together, agreeing in faith about everything. The whole way I go about my day is a full one hundred eighty degrees from what it was. I no longer wonder, *What about me?* or *What am I going to get?* Now it's, *Who can I help? Who can I pray for? Who can I bless?*

I'm tithing. I've never been a consistent tither. The first thing I do when I get money is take out the tithe. Even though I don't have much financial means in the natural right now, I know it's coming and I'm having so much FUN doing it that I almost forget about expecting the harvest part. I'm no longer a Christian in name only and in nominal belief, but I'm finally acting like one in full faith and with bold prayers. No more wimpy Christian life for me. Thank you for being available to God so He could work through you to get to me. —**Oklahoma**

Chapter Two

FAITH Fuels Your Future

It's amazing how much you can do for the Lord and for yourself with faith. The power of personal faith in God is undeniable. It changes you because you can't be saved without faith in God. And, when you put God first and make your faith in Him a part of your life, it changes everything.

Do you know that everything you do and say is recorded by God? Now, that's a powerful statement! But, it is TRUE. All of us will stand before God one day and be judged by what we have done in this life. Now, you shouldn't be afraid of that day. That day will be the most glorious day of your life. Remember, all of your sins will be gone—washed away by the blood of Jesus—and rewards will be given to you for all to see. That ought to make you shout!

Your faith is the element God uses to make you memorable. Think about that! Your faith makes you what you are. It's going to one day be your history for all time. Your past, your present, and your future on this earth will one day be accounted for in Heaven. That's why Hebrews chapter eleven is called "The Hall of Faith" in biblical circles.

I believe God has put things on your heart that He means for you to *have* and also *do*. So, what is *it* that you need and desire? What is *it* that keeps tugging at your heart?

You've Got Enough Faith For It
But if You Don't Know What "IT" is,
Then You Won't Have It!

You are what you believe. You are your faith and that's why *"For by it"* is so important in your life—you can't get a good report without some faith!

If you don't know what *"IT"* is, then you won't have *it*! I know that's a play on words, but it is so true. You have to have faith and use faith because FAITH comes before any other "it" you need or desire—spiritually, physically, financially, or otherwise.

To believe in God is to be convinced of a truth made evident only by revelation.

As believers, our lives are made by revelation, because by turning to God we recognize our place in the entire scheme of things. It puts a lot of other questions to rest and gives us a new perspective on what we can have and do in this life. As His children, we know that who we are is directly related to Who our Father is—and our faith in Him is what changes everything.

Sure, we all have been given the measure of faith—everyone (Romans 12:3). But until we have that revelation about God (where we recognize Him as our Father and accept His love through Christ), we can have no real understanding of our life. Without that revelation, we can't really know our Father. Without faith in Him, we can't even see our lives for what they could be. That revelation is what defines our lives.

Your Faith Sees What Others Can't See
You Have a Road Map that Will Take You Where You Want to Go

Faith in Him is the evidence of things *not* seen. In other words, faith in God gives you "eyes" on the inside—they're spiritual and they help you see spiritual realities that those without faith cannot see or grasp.

The Word tells us the natural man can't comprehend the things of God and considers them foolish. Why? Because the natural man can't "see" what the spiritual man can. The spirit part of man is only perceived by the greatest element ever given to man, and that is FAITH.

**Your faith grasps and recognizes
spiritual realities.
Your faith tests spiritual realities.
Your faith substantiates spiritual realities.**

Now, I know that's a mouthful! So, let me say it this way…your faith is the road map you use on the journey of life. It produces

15

everything you need, desire, and want. You will never be happy in life if you don't use your faith. Without it, you're lost.

That's why plain, old religion is so confusing. It's a dead-end road because it's not really based on faith; it's based on the traditions of other people who had faith. You can't live off the faith of another person. It's got to be personal. So, why travel that dead-end road of religion when you have an interstate system of faith within you that will take you anywhere you want to go?!

Your Faith Will Change
the Way You Think
How Would You Act if You KNEW Nothing Was Impossible?

Faith will make you go where no man has gone before! I know that sounds like Star Trek, but there is a lot of truth to it. You see, faith makes you *think*. It makes you *imagine*. It causes you to *dream*. It's not about wishing. It's an inner hope that begins to surge inside of you and that's a much more active mental process.

When your faith starts to make you think like that, you will start to put your faith into action. Revelation will come from God to you so that you can reach your destination and complete your destiny—and that's what's going to get you that good report! Did you do what God asked you to do? Did you fulfill what He put on your heart? Did you aim to do what's right before Him and spread His Word to others? These are things that only faith in God can accomplish.

You see, God supplies the desire in your heart and He supplies the measure of faith to achieve that desire. Your job is to stir up the faith you've been given and to act on what He said in the Word—and to cast down doubts about His ability to work through you, in you, and around you in order to bring to pass whatever "it" is that you need in your life.

Ask yourself, "How would I act if I knew that nothing was impossible?" When you KNOW that nothing is impossible with God (which is what "faith thinking" is), you will dream, imagine, and act differently. Luke 1:37 says, *"For with God nothing shall be impossible."* Because you have God, He's with you—so, really, nothing is impossible for you.

Tomorrow, here is a simple thing you can do: When you start the day with prayer, add this one thing to your morning—remind yourself that *nothing* is impossible with God. Don't just say it. Meditate on it. Believe it. Then, just see how your emotions change—see how you become instantly focused. Faith pushes out the clutter. Faith streamlines the mind. I like to say it like this...

> **Your faith is a mental uplift.**
> **It's a "fixing" of the soul...a way of directing your**
> **thoughts to the thoughts of Christ.**

Faith is when you put your own will out of your mind and start fixing your thoughts on Jesus. The "mind of Christ" is a mind fueled by pure FAITH IN GOD. What did He say you could do? What did He say you could have? Nothing is impossible with God.

Your Faith Fuels Your Future

Do You Realize that Your Faithfulness Brings Rewards?

I wish I could preach this to you in person! What I'm writing to you is what makes me and this ministry work—faith fuels it all. Now, that's a good report! You see, it's not about being an acquaintance of Christ. It's about having that spiritual face-to-face relationship. I like to call it a vision of Christ in me, the hope of Glory.

Let me go back to the statement I made earlier in this chapter: If you don't know what "IT" is, you will never get *it*. This is about you getting faith and what you desire from God. Those two must work together because, again, if you don't have faith, you can't get what you desire from God. Faith is His currency.

Remember that your faith is what fuels your future. Don't neglect stirring up your faith. Remind yourself that God cannot lie. His Word is true, and whatever it is that is on your heart is possible with God. You can believe the unbelievable and receive the impossible.

Letters come in every week from people telling us that it was the Word of God preached through this ministry that pulled them out of depression, that birthed greater joy in their life, healed their bodies as they reached out in faith, and gave them hope. In other words, the Word preached through this ministry is helping people THINK because we are spreading FAITH!

God does the work, but we must have faith in Him and that's what this ministry does day after day, week after week, and year after year—we preach the Word that builds faith in God. And with God, nothing is impossible for *anyone*.

Chapter Two Faith Declarations

What is *it* that I need and desire?
If I don't have "IT"—faith in God—I'll never have *it*.
"For by it," I access God, knowing that everything I need
and desire comes from Him.

**Why would I travel on the dead-end road of religion
when God has put an interstate system of FAITH
within me that will take me where I want to go?**
Revelations from God come to me.
It's personal—MY faith causes me to think, imagine,
and dream!

**How would I act if I KNEW nothing was impossible
for me?**

I will meditate on this biblical truth today: God is with
me and NOTHING is impossible with God!

**What is keeping me from stirring up my faith and acting
on it today?**

I will cast down every thought that rises up against the
knowledge of God.
He's working *through* me and *in* me to bring every need
and desire of my heart to pass!

Faith Testimony

I asked for prayers for my grandson, age seventeen. He had very complicated brain surgery, then suffered a bleed and stroke three days later. In a coma and on a respirator, there was no hope of his survival or of him living a normal life if he did survive. But God touched him in response to your prayers. He's not only alive, but he is now in rehab and progressing at an unbelievable rate of speed! They expect him to recover full use of his weakened left side and there is no brain damage! Thanks be to God! —**Colorado**

For by
FAITH

Chapter Three
Always TRIUMPH in Christ!

D o you ever wonder, "What is on my report?" I don't know about you, but I'd like to know that! Jesus Himself even once questioned His disciples, *"Whom do men say that I am?"* You see, Jesus knew what was on His divine report—because He knew what His Father said about Him—but He wanted to know what man was saying. That was of interest to Jesus.

What Would it be Like to NEVER Fail?
In Christ, You ALWAYS Triumph

The work Jesus did at the cross forever changed our future as believers. In that work and through our faith and obedience to God, we gain a type of victory that is unalterable and irrevocable.

Do you ever wonder if God will come through for you in the future? Do you wonder what He is doing for you now? Well, in 2 Corinthians 2:14, we learn exactly what God is always going to do for us if we are "in Christ." It says...

"Now thanks be unto God, which always causeth us to triumph in Christ, and maketh manifest the savour of His knowledge by us in every place."

Now, that's a good report! What would it be like if you knew you would never truly fail? Take the long-range view and think about it. Back up for a moment from your own dilemma, if you have one, and allow the magnitude of what Jesus did at the cross to settle into your mind. It forever changed your options…failure is no longer an option for you.

I don't care what it looks like. It can look like failure, but do you realize that that's impossible? Even if you took the "worst-case scenario" that people bring up about those in the Bible who "died in faith," it still isn't failure. They didn't lose. Their everlasting life didn't begin at physical death, it began the moment they accepted Christ. In that split-second decision, they moved to a place called "TRIUMPH" forever and ever. The devil is a liar.

The truth is that you are always destined to win because Christ already won, and so your faith in Him must grow not only to be able to see the long-range view, but also to meet the everyday obstacles of earthly life. You can win at these things, too. But you must ask yourself what you "see" when you see trouble. Notice your mindset, then use the Word to change it if it doesn't line up with triumph!

I love the word "TRIUMPH" because, of course, it dictates a victory. Remember that as believers living "in Christ," our heavenly report has nothing but victory written all over it. Isn't that wonderful?! We need to step back and remind ourselves who

24

we belong to…and who has already won the battle of life. We need to meditate on His words and let them sink into our heart and mind, and let them come out of our mouth. That's how we gain a heavenly perspective. That's how we gain peace.

The Most Important Key to Obtaining a Good Life?
It Is What YOU Believe About Your Future

I love the word "always" in that verse, too. It means there is literally NO failure in a life lived "in Christ." Really think about that. When it comes to you, God has forever linked those two words: "triumph" and "always." You really are a success going somewhere to succeed. Those aren't just "positive" words to think about; they are the life-giving words from God. And the more that you *believe* the Word, the more excited you will be about your future.

In fact, the keys to your good future are found in those three little words from Hebrew 11:2—*"For by it"* or "For by FAITH." Faith changes the way you think about your own life.

You see, everything is always in transition. Life moves forward, it does not move backward. But your mind sometimes wants to get stuck in a moment of time. Sometimes it may want to stay nostalgic and just rethink the past. Sometimes the mind wants to avoid the future. If so, the reason is fear of the future. Why fear when you know you cannot really ever lose?

This is why renewing your mind is so important. It gets you out of your own natural-thinking "head" and into the spiritual-thinking "mind of Christ." This will not only encourage you and lift you up, but also propel you with faith towards your own good future. Courage is born when you "see" the victory. Courage will cause the love for God and His work inside of you to rise up and manifest into actions that bring Him glory. That's why God linked those two words "triumph" and "always" together in 2 Corinthians 2:14.

Remember that God says He will always cause you to triumph if you are "in Christ." Now, that doesn't mean you won't ever have battles in life. After all, how can you "triumph" unless you have some sort of battle? No, the verse means that *in* Christ and *through* Christ (no matter what happens or comes at you in life), you are on a road that leads only one-way: to TRIUMPH.

God Has a Vision for Your Destiny
It's Not Where You Are; It's Where You Are Going

Did you get that? God has a vision for your destiny! And, no, it's not where you are; it's where you're going. Think about that. That's why you are always in transition.

You are going somewhere, and it's a great place. I'm talking about your life and destiny here on this earth and beyond, in Heaven. So, it's vitally important that you refuse a defeated thought-life and, instead, have faith in God. Because it's *"For by it"* that you are going to have the energy and excitement to do what God wants you to do—today, tomorrow, and in the years ahead.

Determine today to align your thoughts with His: *"For I know the thoughts that I think toward you, saith the LORD, thoughts of peace, and not of evil, to give you an expected end"* (Jeremiah 29:11). In other words, triumphing in Christ is your "expected end," so you don't have to live in worry—you can allow yourself to rest in God's good thoughts toward you.

We Must Always Look for Fresh Truths, New Developments, and Extended Horizons

I get up every day always looking forward. I don't want to look back because there's more to do ahead! The Word says, *"Brethren, I count not myself to have apprehended: but this one thing I do, forgetting those things which are behind, and reaching forth unto those things which are before, I press toward the mark for the prize of the high calling of God in Christ Jesus"* (Philippians 3:13-14).

Most preachers always preach about difficulty. I preach about victory. To me, difficulty is just an opportunity to direct and display my energy and my faith in God and myself. Without difficulty, without a trial of some kind, there is no display of faith and fortitude. When things get tough for me, and they do, I think about my soon-coming triumph, my increased faith, and my victory that is on its way.

It's peaceful to know that you are always going to triumph in the end. Faith works—*"For by it"* you relax, knowing that you are more than a conqueror and, in the end, no matter what, you will triumph in Christ. Faith like that allows you the luxury of waking up with joy for the day. Faith like that gives your mind peace so that you can focus on what God has called you to do and have an open heart to help others.

Faith—*"For by it"* you don't just "survive" your own life, but you actually have the peace and passion in your heart to live a good life. The difference is being in Christ and believing in your own good future.

Chapter Three Faith Declarations

 I always TRIUMPH in Christ!

What JESUS did on the cross forever settles my VICTORY.
I am always destined to win because He already won!

I'm growing in FAITH.
"For by it" I see the long-range view of eternal victory, gain a HEAVENLY perspective, and meet the everyday obstacles of life!

 God says He will always cause me to triumph in CHRIST.
I may have battles, but I know that in Christ, I'm ALWAYS on a road that leads to TRIUMPH!

God's DESTINY for me is not where I am—it's where I'm going.
I will align my thoughts with His good Word, have courage, and be at PEACE about my future!

Faith Testimony

I wrote in for prayer while I was still pregnant with my son. I wrote that the doctor had given me a potentially bad report of a mass on my baby's adrenal gland. They even said that it could have been cancerous. But I am writing to tell you that my baby was born not with a cancerous mass, but an edema or bruise on his pancreas. The doctor told me that his body will eventually just absorb it. I took my son for an ultrasound and it is shrinking and pretty soon it will be completely GONE. Praise God! Thank you so much for standing with me in prayer for my son and for the powerful letter you emailed me. It made me so happy to receive it. It helped to keep my faith up. The devil is a liar! —**West Virginia**

Chapter Four

Be a "For by IT" Believer: Live by the Faith of Jesus!

It is so amazing when God gives me brand new insight on familiar scriptures I thought I already knew everything about. Fresh revelation from God always changes your course and destiny in life. And what I have to share with you now is changing the way I view my own faith…and I hope it is a blessing to you.

The words *"For by it"* have been a jumping off point in previous chapters—everything that manifests is *"for by it,"* or by faith. As I often say: "If you don't understand *IT,* you'll never get *it.*"

The Big "IT" of FAITH Will Bring You All the Other "its" of Life

What's the big *IT?* FAITH! What's the little *it?* The manifestation of whatever it is that you want, need, and desire from God in this life. It takes the big IT—FAITH, *"For by it"*—to get the little "its" of life that you want from the Lord.

Be Crucified with Christ…
It Will Enable You to Live by HIS Faith

Now, I want to build upon that by going to another very familiar passage about faith…

> *"I am crucified with Christ: nevertheless I live; yet not I, but Christ liveth in me: and the life which I now live in the flesh **I live by the faith of the Son of God**, Who loved me, and gave Himself for me."* (Galatians 2:20)

That scripture is packed with insight, and what I want to focus on today is realizing that this verse shows us that we can live by "the faith of the Son of God." Think about that! This is talking about living by *Jesus'* faith!

Jesus' faith was produced by His energy of Spirit. He only said what He heard the Father say. If you want to walk and live by "the faith of the Son of God," then you should not only believe His way, but also do what He did, too. In other words, we must always aim to trust and honor God and always speak God's Word. It doesn't matter what's happening—God's Word changes our perspective and has the power to change our circumstances.

Jesus' faith is a grasping of Almighty power. Whatever God tells you to do will have power in it—power to do impossible things. Proverbs 1:33 says, *"But whoso hearkeneth unto Me shall dwell safely, and shall be quiet from fear of evil."* In other words, failure is not an option when you walk by the faith of the Son of God. If Jesus' faith worked for Him, you know that it will work for you, too.

Be Strong...Speak the Word and Stay in the Right Environment

What are you believing for? What do you want? It will come to pass if you stick with the faith of the Son of God. Now, for you to be able to stick with His faith, you must study the Word for yourself and speak it...but you must also keep yourself in the right environment. And that right environment is the right church where the Word of God is taught.

The right environment includes being under the right authority—you'd be surprised how lost you can get putting yourself under the tutelage of a preacher who has no faith in God or no respect for His righteous Word. You'd be surprised how many unbelieving pastors and Christians there are out there. Their churches may have a lot of people in them, but how strong are those people? Do they know the truth? Have they been taught enough of the Word to understand how to "fight the good fight" of faith? Are they capable of "rightly dividing the Word of truth" or are they easily swayed by every doctrine that comes along in Christian circles? Again, the question really is how *strong* are they?

I promise you, when Satan attacks a Christian who has not gained much strength, they will succumb to whatever the attack is—they will literally buckle under whatever the devil is trying to do to them and in their life. I've seen it happen so many times. When that believer goes to the pastor who schooled him in his weakness to ask why, that believer will hear a faithless cliché like, "Well, you know how God is...sometimes He does and sometimes He don't!"

33

It is sad, but that's a church hearing the words of a leader who is not "living by the faith of the Son of God." A person of real faith will encourage you to put your trust and faith in God, they will not train you to be weak. A person of real faith will not guide you towards faithlessness.

Be a Person of Conviction...
A Grain of Conviction is Worth More than a Trainload of Opinion!

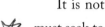

It is not sufficient just to know the Bible intellectually; you must seek to know it in SPIRIT and in TRUTH. Are you getting this? Many people know a lot about Scripture, but all they do is debate it and express their opinion about it. They miss the whole point and live in turmoil instead of peace because they have no real faith in their Father God and they have no real faith in His Word. It's just another thing to debate. The faith of the Son of God that Paul was talking about in Galatians 2:20 is NOT that kind of faith!

This kind of faith produces convictions, not just opinions. A grain of conviction is worth more than a trainload of religious opinion. Glory! We live by faith, we walk by faith, we are sanctified by faith, we are kept by faith, and we overcome by faith! Now, that's the kind of faith that Paul was talking about when he spoke of the faith of Jesus, and it's that faith—Jesus' faith—that is working in us. It's in us!

Be Consistent…Focus on the Goals of Your Heart and You Will Always Be "Up"

I know you will accomplish everything you said you would do. You ought to put that saying on something, somewhere in your house so that you see it every day: "I will accomplish everything I said I would do!" Make it personal. Make yourself a list. Talk to God about it each day when you see it. Thank Him for the faith within you that was given to you by the sacrifice of His Son, Jesus. Remind yourself daily (not just on Sunday) that you WILL accomplish everything you said you'd do!

This kind of faith will lead to a rich and abundant fellowship with God Almighty. Through repetition—by reminding yourself of exactly what God has put in you (the same faith that Jesus had, His faith) and by consistently focusing on the goals that He has put on your heart (daily, not just on Sunday)—you will find that you will always be "up" when everyone around you may seem down.

The Word will lift your heart and strengthen your faith. Keeping your focus on Who is inside of you and what He has said in His Word will help you clear out the doubt. And, keeping those goals you want to reach in front of your face daily will stimulate you and inspire you to keep on moving forward in faith and in action.

You can live like this! Defeat doesn't have to be in your vocabulary. You can live by faith every day, like Jesus did when He walked on the earth.

Chapter Four Faith Declarations

I'm a "For by IT" Believer—I live by the faith of Jesus!

I'm a "For by IT" Believer—I will accomplish everything I said I would do!

I'm Crucified with Christ—I'm living by the faith of the Son of God!

I'm Strong—I'm speaking the Word and staying in the right environment!

I'm a Person of Conviction—Conviction is worth more than a trainload of opinion!

I'm Consistent—I focus on my goals and look forward with faith!

I'm a Messenger of Salvation and Hope—I help others to live by faith, too!

Faith Testimony

Six months ago I requested prayer for my friend who was in a battle with lung cancer. We all stood in agreement for her healing, drawing on the power of the blood of Jesus. Her scan came back and the doctor said he saw no more reason to continue the chemo! The tumor was gone! Thank You, Jesus, and thanks to all of your prayer warriors. God is good and He loves His children. JDM has been such a blessing to me! —**Texas**

For by
FAITH

Chapter Five

Looking Unto JESUS...
The Author and Finisher of
Our FAITH

D on't you just love the Word of God?! When I think back to before I was saved, I don't know how I made it. I believe it was only God's love for me while I was a "chief of sinners" that kept me safe from the hand of the enemy. Thank God for His love!

I shouldn't be writing this to you—but because of *His* love and grace towards me when I was yet a sinner, I am writing it. I believe you probably feel the same way about your past, too. By the love and grace of God, you are here!

If You Want to Live a Life of Faith...LOOK TO JESUS

Everything worth doing or having in life is accessed by faith in God. He is where ALL good things come from—whether they are spiritual, physical, financial, or in any other way, He is the Source.

I want to go to a phrase from Scripture that I believe tells us what we have to do in order to *start* having faith, and also what we should do in order to *finish* well in life—like those elders who obtained a good report. How do we do this? Hebrews 12:2 gives us the answer when it says...

 "Looking unto Jesus, the Author and Finisher of our faith..."

This is such a powerful phrase in Scripture that I believe it should be the focus of this chapter. It's an invaluable tip. As for yourself, where are you looking? Are you looking unto Jesus? Where is your focus?

Remind yourself that only Jesus is the "Author" and "Finisher" of your faith—so how can you "start" without Him or how can you "finish" anything of value without Him?

 In the original language, these words meant that Jesus was the captain or leader—the "perfecter" of our faith. In other words, Jesus has top ranking. Jesus is the pattern by which we live.

If You Want to Put the Past Behind You...
LOOK TO JESUS

You may remember that in my last chapter I talked about Paul and how he described the life of faith. Paul was passionate about his salvation. Paul knew it not only gave him access to God and a clean slate where he could put the past behind him, but it also gave him the ability to access God in everyday life and through big challenges.

Paul considered himself a dead man when it came to his old life and his past. He really focused on having the faith of Jesus—not relying on himself but relying on the One in his heart. He aligned himself so much with Jesus that he said, *"I am crucified with Christ: nevertheless I live...and the life which I now live in the flesh I live by the faith of the Son of God"* (Galatians 2:20).

What was Paul doing? He was "looking unto Jesus" for everything. That's how he put down his flesh and lived a new life. He lived each day by a FAITH higher than his own—by the faith of the Son of the living God Who loved him and died for him. Jesus became the center-point of Paul's life.

God had a plan for Paul's life—a huge plan. To fulfill that plan, all Paul had to really do was that one thing: He had to keep *"Looking unto Jesus, the Author and Finisher of our faith."* The same is true for you.

Can you live every day in the "natural" by the faith of Jesus like Paul did? Yes! And the way to put the past behind you and live the "crucified life" that Paul talked about is the same, regardless of God's plan for your life. All you have to do is keep *"Looking unto Jesus, the Author and Finisher of our faith."*

No matter what God's plan is for YOUR life, that's what you have to do.

If You Want Wisdom and Guidance for YOUR Life...
LOOK TO JESUS

The more we consider the life of Jesus, the more clearly we see the demands of His calling in life—demands that He agreed to.

41

Jesus made it really clear that He said and did only what He heard from His Father, God. In other words, Jesus stuck to God's plan for His life. He let God lead Him and didn't follow every whim.

Now, if *we* are to live by *His* faith, then we must know how to walk in that kind of faith in our everyday life—and that takes wisdom. The Word of God is full of wisdom. The Holy Spirit is also within you and able to lead and guide you.

You may have heard me say this many times, but I feel led to share it with you again:

Jesus is the Author and Finisher of our faith, but He is under no responsibility to finish something He has not authored.

This is why preachers get into so much trouble at times. Many either don't stop and really look at the demands of their calling or they imagine much larger demands and do things in their own strength. I'll give you an example of this.

Have you ever been to a church that started a building program and got into financial trouble? Then the pastor had to cut back on his staff and really start pushing the congregation to give more money every Sunday. What happened? Well, it's possible that God didn't "author" that building program at all. The Word warns us to "count the cost" before we "build the tower." In other words, faith is not "winging it" and God is not responsible for finishing things He didn't author. Now, this might make somebody mad, but it doesn't change the truth.

You see, that building program might have been a good idea but was it a *God*-idea? On a side note, you might ask how you can tell the difference, looking from the natural, whether a project is a "good" idea or a "God" idea. Time usually tells. People will grow weary with a good idea and walk out on it, but a God-idea will produce a passion in people toward the completion of that project.

When God is into something, a "holy anxiety" comes over people to finish it. It's so easy to recognize. You know God is the author of that. And if He is, then guess what? He has the responsibility to finish it. Glory!

If You Want to Live a Life of Assured Confidence... LOOK TO JESUS

You can use this "passion toward completion" when it comes to what the Word says about healing for your body, salvation for your family, prosperity in your finances, or anything else. The reason this ministry is blessed is because we have the passion for completion and a holy anxiety. You see, I know in Whom I have believed and I'm persuaded. I know God has called me in this ministry. I know God is going to bless me, and I will finish this race!

Now, that brings me to my next point...

Faith is a life of assured confidence in an unseen future!

It looks like I'm starting to preach in this book! Don't let time defeat you. If you haven't seen what you are "faith-ing" manifest yet, don't give up. Your faith is still working. LOOK TO JESUS! The evidence of your faith is "not seen"—spiritually, physically, or financially—but mark my words, in the very near future you will say, "And it came to pass!"

Don't you just love that phrase in Scripture? It's all over the Bible. Testimony after testimony in the Word shows how faith brings results. Unseen faith creates "concrete evidence" of the power of our God. Read the Gospels and see the miracles and unusual things that happened for people who were willing to look to Jesus with fearless faith. There is an assured confidence that comes from looking to Jesus and living by His faith. Don't "try" it…live it!

If You Want to Make God Proud…
LOOK TO JESUS

What matters the most to God? People! How do I know that? Because what matters most to the Father is the same as it has been since He sent His only begotten Son, Jesus: God wants souls. His Son, Jesus, gave up His heavenly privileges and took on the demands of His earthly calling for the cause of reaching *people* for the Father.

God cares about every person—every soul. I believe that nothing makes God more proud than when we accept His gift of salvation, take on His nature, use the faith of His Son, and start caring about people, too. If you want to make God proud, all you have to do is look to Jesus, see what He gave up so that people could find God. He gave His life—what more could He give?

Each of us can do our part and make God proud. We can

fulfill His plan for our lives and fill up Heaven, too! We can keep spreading His goodness throughout the world.

We can keep *"Looking unto Jesus, the Author and Finisher of our faith."* It's the BEST way to live!

Chapter Five Faith Declarations

I Look to Jesus—He is the Author and Finisher of my faith!

I Look to Jesus—He puts my past behind me and grants me new life!

I Look to Jesus—He gives me wisdom and guidance like no other!

I Look to Jesus—He keeps me focused and gives me passion!

I Look to Jesus—He fills me with assured confidence!

I Look to Jesus—He gives me His faith and His heart for people!

Faith Testimony

I wanted to share with everyone the miraculous and awesome things that God has done for me. I was in a motorcycle wreck in 2010 and was told I would be a vegetable. But because of the power of your prayers and God's holy, healing hands, I can do almost everything that I used to do! I got spinal cancer in 2012 and couldn't walk, but, once again, our Father saved me and I am cancer free! In accordance with Mark 11:23-24, the mountain in my path has been moved! Thank you for your prayers. —**Oklahoma**

For by
FAITH

Chapter Six

Faith is More than Believing—It's DOING

A s I've said, when it comes to gaining whatever it is that you desire from God, if you don't know what "**IT**" is, then you won't get *it*! Spiritually, physically, financially or in any other area, you need faith *in* God to receive anything *from* God. For by "IT"—FAITH—you inherit all the promises of God. For by "IT"—FAITH—you access all that God has for you.

We Are the Trustees of FAITH
Faith is More than Believing—It's DOING

The truth of the New Testament is that faith is here for us to USE. It's never dead if you are using it to do something. You were given the measure of faith (portion) and it's always ready to be used.

Faith is here NOW, always and forever. So, my point is this: **Whether we like it or not, we are called to be the trustees of faith to mankind.**

Think about that for a moment. Being a "trustee of faith" is an awesome responsibility. God literally entrusts His message and His Spirit to us to pass along. God trusts you and me to not just talk about what we believe, but also to show the world that, by faith, they can see His Word come to pass.

We Are in that Great "Cloud of Witnesses"
Faith is Letting Go of What Holds Us Back—It's RUNNING!

God has given us—our generation—the task to complete the work that the "cloud of witnesses" in Scripture began. That's why Hebrews 12:1 is so important. It says…

"Wherefore seeing we also are compassed about with so great a cloud of witnesses, let us lay aside every weight, and the sin which doth so easily beset us, and let us run with patience the race that is set before us."

Now, running the race with patience is a big job. In fact, "the race" is why I preach this Gospel. Every day there are people who are hurting and need to find God and, as I often say, the only Jesus some people may ever see is the Jesus in you or the Jesus in me. So, running the race is much too important of a job to become lazy. It's too important to get sidetracked.

Things will always come up in life that try and weigh us down. Things will come up that tempt us to sin and to stop moving forward in our faith. The Word warns us that these things can "easily beset us"—or in other words, hold us back or stop us from running. God warns us so that we can be aware that things will come up all the time, but all we need to do is "lay aside" those things as they come up.

Why does God encourage us to "lay aside" what might try and hold us back? Because He wants us to make some headway in this great vision. God wants people to come to the knowledge of Him. God wants us to show others what it means to love, serve, and live by faith in God.

Notice that the word "patience" is pointed out in that verse, too. That warns us that patience is going to be something we need in order to move forward. So, be aware that you'll need it each day.

As things come up, remember that God wouldn't tell you to do something you are unable to do. With Him, you can "lay aside" things. With Him, you can "run with patience" each day. Remember what I said in previous chapters, "all you need is faith for today!" The same goes with patience. Just concentrate on today.

The Eyes of the Multitudes Are On US
Faith is Using the Power of the *"Mind of Christ"—It's THINKING!*

Remember that "today" is the day of salvation for somebody. Who knows? Maybe you'll be the one to lead them onto God's path. Maybe you'll be the one who shows them what it means to be a person of faith. Maybe, through what you say and do, they'll put aside their preconceived notions of what it means to be a Christian and open their heart to God.

So many eyes are upon us. The eyes of multitudes—past and present—are upon us. That's why we're called "trustees." God believes in you and me. He knows we can get the job done! Isn't that wonderful? He has faith in us and we have faith in Him. So, my second point is this: **As the trustees of faith, we are bringing in the final age of mankind.**

We are living in the age of Jesus Christ. We are not beginning things; we are only carrying them on. That's why God has given us access to the mind of Christ—and it is a powerful mind that brings with it strong convictions and a firm will.

I stake all faith, all truth, and all hope on that power—Christ's power. The power of the mind of Christ is what causes me to think, imagine, and dream higher. There is no clutter in the mind of Christ, so there doesn't need to be clutter in our minds either. If we abide in Him and His Word abides in us, our minds will become streamlined. We will become people who are more peaceful, more hopeful, more excited, and more energetic about living this life well and affecting more and more lives for good.

We Run Together and We Don't Stop
Faith is Confident and Encouraging—It's SPEAKING!

Together, we can touch the world for Jesus. Together, we can and will get their bodies healed. Together, we can teach them God's principles to get out of debt and stay out!

Now, when you make it personal like that, it shows that you have strong confidence in God. "For by IT"—FAITH—you know that the Word cannot and will not return unto Him void. It will go forth and produce. So, my third point is: **We must never let our confidence in God be misplaced. There are too many witnesses watching.**

As believers, we are running the race together. We are connected by our faith in God and our love for the world that He sent Christ to save. So if one gets weak, we carry them. We aren't called to stop moving forward. We aren't called to criticize each other. No, we are called to encourage each other, to reach down and carry each other, and to keep moving.

We are trustees of faith and we are advancing the Kingdom. We are winning souls and helping others find hope, strength, faith, and success through the Word. In other words, we are accomplishing what God has told us to do, and we're doing it together. Glory!

This is why the Word says, *"Let the weak say, I am strong"* (Joel 3:10). God wants us to encourage ourselves in the truth, regardless of how we feel. He wants us to not just think it and not just believe it; He wants us to SAY it.

I love that Romans 4:17 says to *call* those things that "be not" as though they *were*. Speaking in faith—that's what made Abraham the man he was. That's what makes us who we are. And we learned it all from our God Who was the first to call those things that be not as though they were until they are! You see, we are all partners together in faith.

We Didn't Begin It, But We Continue It
Faith is Carrying the Message to the World—It's SHARING!

We must not loiter or linger in this vision to advance the Kingdom. We must not walk with measured steps because we are "compassed about" with a great cloud of witnesses. We didn't begin things, but we are carrying them on. We are in the age of Jesus Christ and We are trustees of faith. We must continue to *"Go ye into all the world, and preach the Gospel to every creature"* because this is what Jesus asked us to do…and we can't help but share what He has given us.

We will continue to have FAITH in His Word and see all God's promises to us fulfilled. Everywhere we go, we can be the ones to show others how GOOD God is!

Chapter Six Faith Declarations

My Faith is More than Believing—*It's DOING!*

I Am a Doer—I don't just talk about the Word, I do what it says.

I Am a Soul-Winner—I'm running the race set before me with patience.

I Am a Trustee of Faith—I'm in that great *"cloud of witnesses."*

I Am Focused—I lay aside every weight and sin that tries to stop me.

I Am Confident—I call those things that be not as though they were.

I Am Encouraging—I lift up others and speak with truth and strength.

I Have the Mind of Christ—It's powerful, peaceful, and clutter-free.

I Am a "Go Ye!" Believer—I didn't begin the work, but I'm carrying it on.

Faith Testimony

I asked you to pray for my friend. He has been out of work for over a year taking treatments for a liver condition. He wasn't given a good chance to live. Not only is he is back to work now, but the doctors can't find anything wrong with his liver! Every time I see him go by, I say, "Thank You!" and "Praise You, Lord!" Thank you so much for faithful prayers. —**Tennessee**

Chapter Seven

Your FREEDOM Starts with a Choice—Make It!

No matter what country you call home, you can make a choice to be free...and I'm not talking about politics. I'm talking about a freedom that goes beyond man-made borders and ideas. I'm talking about TRUE freedom that can only be had in Christ. Whom the Son has set free is *what*? Free indeed (John 8:36). Glory!

You see, faith makes you free. Faith is how you get a "good report" with God. Faith is how you draw those unseen things you hope for into reality. "For by IT" (faith), you will gain whatever "it" is that you are believing for—spiritually, physically, financially, or in any other area. Faith in God that is active and real produces results. But, "If you don't know what IT is, you won't have it!" Developing your faith in God is critical to getting the needs and desires of your heart met.

The part of "IT" (faith) that I want to share on in this chapter is freedom.

Freedom is Your CHOICE—Take It!

Isn't it wonderful to be free?! But what made you free? It was your CHOICE to believe in what God did when He sent His only begotten Son to die for you—that choice is what redeemed you. The blood was there all along, but you couldn't be free until you made a choice.

The same is true with all the stumbling blocks of life that God has freed you of or wants to free you from. Freedom begins when you make a choice to believe what the Word says about you and the life you can have, instead of what the circumstances say and what your eyes see. Freedom starts with a choice.

The free will to choose is a great gift that God has given to each of us. In Deuteronomy 30:19, God asked Israel to choose something, and that something was life and blessing or death and cursing. You can't separate one from the other. If you choose life, you get blessing. If you choose death, you get cursing.

Did you notice that although God gave the people a choice, He expressly pointed out the right choice? You may ask, "Why?" Well, because God is a good God and He created us to be free. We were not created to be independent of God, but free in our soul—and only the choice of life and blessing contains that kind of freedom. The choice of death and cursing does not bring a life of freedom. That choice only brings confinement.

God is Giving You Divine Advice—Take It

When God is giving you divine advice, I suggest you take it. Yet it's amazing to me how many people go the wrong way. Divine advice is as good as it gets!

Why would anyone choose sickness over health? Poverty over prosperity? Death over life? I could go on and on. Yet, as amazing as it is, so many people in both the church and out in the world do make those choices.

I personally like to choose what has been suggested by God— and that is life and blessing. So, why do so many people not take God's advice? Maybe they just haven't read the Word enough to know the good life when they see it. Maybe they are still clinging to old feelings of unworthiness. Maybe they just have been captive for so long that they are literally comfortable with the wrong choices and actually fear being free. There are so many reasons why, but if we all only knew how wonderful life could be if we simply took God's advice, I believe each of us would step forward and make the right choice every single time. Choice is involved in everything we do. So what does it take to make that choice of life and blessing? One thing: a decision!

Never Debate What God Tells You to Choose— Accept It

My next point is this: A choice always turns a debate into a decision. Never debate what God tells you to choose. Accept by

59

faith that by His stripes you are healed (1 Peter 2:24), even though your eyes can't see it yet and you don't feel well. That's making a decision to have faith and choose life.

I'm not telling you to deny how you feel. That's not faith, that's just denial. No, I'm telling you to choose what you *want* (which is to feel good) rather than choose what you *have* (which is feeling bad). You see, your faith will go to work on whatever you decide to choose. Did you get that?

Faith works on your choice. Your destiny will be determined by what you say and do. Now, that's the truth! The Word tells us that the truth will set us free—but not just the truth on its own, but the truth that we *know*. In other words, "*For by it*" (faith in God and His Word), we are set free.

Isn't that word "freedom" just beautiful? It lifts you just hearing it and thinking about it. That's because feeling free, even for a moment, feels good. But *knowing* that the truth has made you free and walking in that freedom, well, that is what keeps changing your life for the better, because that's faith in God.

Freedom, the Sweetest Part of Faith—Receive It

Why do people like sugar? They like it because it's sweet. It just tastes good! Faith through freedom is one of the parts of God that tastes good. That's why I follow after God every day. The psalmist David wrote, "*My soul followeth hard after thee*" (Psalm 63:8). I can relate, because that's me! I love the Lord and His work with every fiber of my being.

To me, the work of the ministry is not hard. No, it is sweet. I love seeing people get saved, healed, blessed, and changed by the Lord's message. Why? Because I love seeing them find freedom. That is what they are getting from the Lord in many varying ways. His truth sets people FREE!

Faith is Meant to Be Spread Around—Share It

Everybody on this planet will have a chance to obtain a good report simply by having faith in God. Our job as believers, once we hear the message, is to spread the message so that others can find faith and freedom too. It's a sweet honor to give others that opportunity.

When the Founding Fathers of the United States signed the Declaration of Independence, we as a people were free. Yes, we had to fight a war. Yes, it was not easy. Yes, it was tiresome at times. But it produced a nation that changed the way the peoples of the world thought.

"For by it" (faith), man has the freedom to choose what's good or what's not—because we are ALL made in the image of God. We can take this faith and give it to the world—in other words, we can spread it around! When we do that, the Holy Spirit takes the Word of God that we share and draws people into freedom. The Holy Spirit of God compels them to come in. He is the One Who does the work in them, but He lets you and me have a part in sharing freedom. We are His hands, His mouth, and His feet.

61

We are bringing real freedom to people all over this earth and it is beautiful.

> *"And how shall they preach, except they be sent? As it is written, How beautiful are the feet of them that preach the Gospel of peace, and bring glad tidings of good things!"* (Romans 10:15)

Chapter Seven Faith Declarations

I know the TRUTH! I choose to BE FREE!

Being FREE is the sweetest part of faith—I'm tasting it!
I choose to "taste and see" every day that God is good.

The TRUTH sets me free—I'm not debating it!
I choose to ACCEPT what God says.

Freedom starts with a CHOICE—I'm making it!
I can have what the Word says I can have.

What I'm believing for WILL come to pass—I'm speaking it!
I don't deny circumstances. I choose to have faith.

Divine ADVICE is as good as it gets—I'm taking it!
I choose LIFE and BLESSING every day. It's God's will for me.

Faith should be SPREAD AROUND—I'm sharing it!
I choose to give others the opportunity to find faith and be free.

Faith Testimony

In March 2006, Jesse came to our church. I'd had an ectopic pregnancy and multiple miscarriages for three years. At the end of service, he called out, "Someone here is having problems getting pregnant." I JUMPED over people to get to the front. He said, "Now, I have a blessing of multiplication and increase in my life, so once I pray for you, you have to decide when to stop." I had no more miscarriages and have had three babies since. We have now stopped. I knew in my heart that Brother Jesse was right—they'd just keep coming and three was enough for me! Now when Jesse visits our church, my husband is now the Children's Pastor there and gets to help Jesse out before, during, and after service as Pastoral Usher. It's a great night for our entire family! Last year, we got to introduce all of our towheaded children to Jesse and thank him for being open to what God is trying to accomplish in his services! —**Missouri**

Chapter Eight

Don't Give Up on Your Faith

The most precious thing you have in life is your faith. Now, notice this: faith is the substance that has gotten you everything you possess right now in the spiritual, physical, and financial world. Faith is precious! Yet the church world doesn't value faith the way faith should be valued. Think about that for a minute.

When Jesus Comes Back, He'll Be Looking for FAITH
Shall He Find IT on the Earth?

Jesus asked an astounding question in Luke 18:8: *"When the Son of Man cometh, shall He find faith on the earth?"* This question has always bothered me. I'd think, *Why would He say that?!* Now, after 36 years of full-time ministry, I know why.

The Church at times has attacked faith with such a vengeance. They've called it hyper or Gnosticism, and are willing to call it just about anything else they can think of that will discourage people from using it. Well, let me tell you what "it" really is! It is LIFE for you, your children, and your children's children. It is the FUTURE of who we are in Christ.

65

The source and secret of faith is our conception of God's character, whether we are conscious of it or not.

Our ideas about God are what determine our loyalty to Him. As for me, there is nothing left for me in this world but God. That's why I preach the Gospel every chance I can.

People Will Do Almost Anything but WAIT
Are You "Fertilizing" Your Human Nature?

Time means nothing to me anymore. If I'm believing by faith for something and it happens quickly, fine. If it doesn't happen quickly, that's fine also. I will never let time defeat me.

Time will not make me misjudge the God I serve.

There are people in the world who can be relied upon to do almost anything except wait! Isn't that the truth? Waiting destroys them every time, but it should not. Let me give you a revelation:

No seed takes longer to grow than the seed sown in the soil of human nature.

Human nature does not want to humble itself in prayer and it does not want to wait on anything—but God requires these things. The reason why no seed takes longer to grow than the seed sown in the soil of human nature is because God created us to be filled with *His* nature. We have to "fertilize" our human nature with His nature. How do we do that? With prayer. When we quit praying, our faith starts to die. Yet, in order to pray, we must have faith. So, let me say it this way:

Faith pours forth prayer and the pouring forth of the heart in prayer gives steadfastness to faith.

Did you get that? The reason I believe faith is above all spiritual graces is because faith is the organ by which we accept both revelation and grace. The reason God has been telling me to use Hebrews 11:1-2 as the foundation for this book is because FAITH is what Jesus will be looking for when He comes back to this earth.

When Jesus comes back (and He will), I know He will find FAITH—because He will find it in believers like you and me! We aren't giving up on what He taught and what He lived. We aren't giving up on Who He is and how He works. We are going to fertilize our nature with the power of prayer. We're going to learn that since time cannot stop the Word of God from coming to pass, we won't let it discourage us or make us give up on our faith. God is God. He is faithful. He will do what He said in His Word—spiritually, physically, and financially—if we apply it in faith.

I also believe that when Jesus comes back, He will not only find faith, but also love, joy, and everything else that the body of Christ should have. We are a family. If we go to God in faith and in prayer, our Father will always be faithful to pour out His Spirit and His ways in us.

All the fruit of His Spirit can flow in us if we go to Him and keep fertilizing! It'll flow down from Heaven into our heart and out to this world—and that is exactly what God wants us to do. Evangelism is about letting Him flow to the world. It's about being God's hands, feet, and voice in the earth.

We Can All Make Jesus "Irresistible"
Inspire Devotion to Jesus and Strike Fear in Satan's Camp!

Not long ago, I got a word from the Lord from a pastor in Canada that blessed me so much. She said, "Jesse, you make Jesus irresistible!" I shouted inside and out! I've been feasting on it ever since because this is what I believe God wants all of us to be like when we share Christ with others, either by witnessing or just by letting our light shine.

In fact, that word made me think about the two things that I always aim to do when I preach the Word: 1) I want to inspire devotion to Jesus in people and 2) I want to strike fear in Satan's camp. I believe I do both. I make sure there is a lot of noise in the camp of God! We must be a powerful force against Satan and his cohorts.

Irresistible is what God is and He lives in us. And it's only by faith that we go to Him in prayer and get filled with His glorious light. It's God's plan to use each and every one of us. Through us, those who are living in darkness will be irresistibly drawn to the Light of the World—Jesus Christ!

Chapter Eight Faith Declarations

I won't give up on my faith!

I AM LOYAL—I know that God will accomplish everything He promised to me.

I AM PATIENT—I will never let time make me misjudge the God I serve.

I AM HUMBLE—I will always bow my head and pray in faith to my Lord.

I AM STEADFAST—I will always "fertilize" my nature with His nature in prayer.

I AM BOLD—I am His hands and feet on this earth and I will not hide my faith.

 I AM IRRESISTIBLE—The Light of the World is Jesus and He shines through me.

Faith Testimony

I wrote requesting prayer for my grandson, whom the doctors said was brain dead. We never gave up. He woke up and remembered everything! We are shouting the glory to God: he is healed! Thanks for praying with us. —**Maryland**

Chapter Nine

It's a Question of Faith "Do you believe that I am able to do this?" – Jesus

Faith in God is such a vast subject. I believe that we will never get through it all, even in Heaven. Without faith, it's impossible not only to please God but also to access Him and have your needs and desires met by Him. So you must *believe*. Believe what? Believe that He is God and He is ABLE.

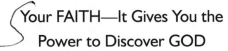

Your FAITH—It Gives You the Power to Discover GOD
It Makes You Ready to Receive God's Best

Faith is so personal. The reason we need to understand more about it is because our individual faith is the only thing we have that gives us the divine power to discover God. Through our faith, we discover who He is, what He does, and His methods of communicating, educating, and blessing His children—all things we need to know.

Faith gives you the ability to touch God Almighty. Now, that's important! God wants to do so much for you, and He uses *your* faith to bring all the things He wants to do for you to pass. So, let's get to my first point in this chapter: **The spirit of faith is the spirit that gets us ready to receive God's best blessings**.

God doesn't just want you to be better—He wants you to be the BEST! He is interested in your development the most. So, do you want to discover a little more about Him today? Because I have a story from the Gospel of Matthew about two blind men that I believe just might "open your eyes" too!

Your FAITH—It Gives You the Passion to Cry Out
It Gives You the Tenacity to Follow Through

The miraculous story of the two blind men is found in Matthew 9:27-31 (NKJV) and it takes place during the earthly ministry of Jesus. You see, reports of His healing power were spreading like wildfire and so, as Jesus was leaving one town, Matthew 9:27 tells us that two blind men followed after Him so that they could be healed, too. These two men not only *followed* Jesus, but the Scripture says that they also *cried out* to Him, saying, *"Son of David, have mercy on us!"* They were passionate about receiving not only healing, but also mercy. In other words, "Lord, see our plight! Your mercy will save us from what we have become."

Next, the Word says that Jesus stopped and walked into the house and the two men kept following him until they *"came to Him"* (vs. 28). Jesus is the same yesterday, today, and forever—He always responds to cries for mercy from those who have the humility to acknowledge who He is. Another point about Jesus to notice is that

He stopped walking so they could catch up. He is no respecter of persons and will be faithful to wait for you and me to draw close to Him, too.

That brings me to a point about the blind men—**they didn't give up.** These two men were passionate in crying out and persistent in following through. They kept moving towards Jesus until they had gone from *outside* the edge of the city to *inside* the house—a place where they were positioned in His presence. Faith brings the will to follow-through and a strong desire to get close to the Lord.

Your FAITH—It Gives You the Guts to Answer Jesus Honestly
He Asks, "Do You Believe that I Am Able to Do This?"

Next, Jesus asked the men point-blank and bluntly, *"Do you believe that I am able to do this?"* (vs. 28). Now, think about that! It is the very first thing Jesus says. And He didn't move until they answered His question. Jesus never asked, "Do you think I'm *willing* to do this?" He didn't just immediately heal them either—even though they had already asked for mercy and recognized His position as the Son of David.

So, what was He looking for with this question? He was looking for FAITH. The kind of faith that was eager enough to cry out, follow Him, acknowledge Him, and draw close. The kind of faith that had ears to hear and wouldn't be offended by the question, *"Do you believe I am able to do this?"* The kind of faith that would assess itself and answer honestly.

The men responded with just two words: *"Yes, Lord."* (vs. 28). Simple, total agreement—notice that. We are talking about two men and one Jesus. It's called the prayer of agreement and it's a powerful thing! The faith of two and the divinity of One brings what? Manifestation.

"Then He touched their eyes…" (vs. 29). The point? What they *did*, what they *believed*, and what they *said* caused Jesus' hand to reach out.

Your FAITH—It Opens Your Eyes to the Miracle of Truth
Nothing Happens Unless You Believe Jesus is Able

Jesus not only reached out and touched their eyes, but at the same moment, He told them exactly HOW the miracle would happen:

> *"According to your faith be it done unto you."*
>
> (Matthew 9:29 ASV)

That's right. Jesus refused to take credit for the healing! But He did make sure to do the questioning, the touching, and the simple one-line teaching of truth that brought them to the point of receiving. I want you to notice that those blind eyes did not pop open and see until the men heard those nine words of truth: *"According to your faith be it done unto you."*

Your FAITH—All of Us Need to "Hear" More of the Word
Strengthen Your Faith and
Catch Up to Your Ability to Ask

One of the great morals of this miraculous story is this: **Their faith was tested in the touch of Jesus.**

All of us will have our faith tested by the Lord. When we ask for something from Jesus, it's very likely that we'll have to answer the question, *"Do you believe I am able to do this?"* Jesus would not want us to pretend and lie about it (whatever it might be that we are asking of Him),but He would want us to stretch ourselves and do what we need to do to strengthen our faith in His ability to "do this."

If you have ever wondered why we sometimes don't receive what we need or desire from the Lord, I hope you will think and pray about my next point: **We each have the ability to ask God to do anything, but sometimes our faith is not ready to receive what we ask for.**

The truth is that sometimes we just don't have the strength in our faith to receive it—we aren't convinced that God is able to do "this" for us. Oh, we know He can do it. But the thing we are asking Him for seems so big, so hard-to-do, or so impossible that our mind fills with doubt and worry. The eyes of our heart move from Jesus to the problem, and land squarely on the problem.

The promises of God must be larger than the problems you are facing, because what you focus your faith on is what you will have.

So if the problem is what has your attention and all your belief, then that problem will continue being a problem for you. Don't use your faith for what you already have—that problem! Use your faith for what you want—the mercy of Jesus to help you resolve it at the very root.

I believe that God wants all of us to have the honest and childlike faith that changes things and the bold and open faith that moves mountains! That's why the Word tells us so plainly how to build our faith: *"Faith comes by hearing, and hearing by the Word of God"* (Romans 10:17 NKJV).

All of us need to "hear" more of the Word! Regardless of what we are facing spiritually, physically, financially, or in any other way, the more we hear, the more we will be able to say from our heart, "Yes, Lord. You are able!"

Your FAITH—It's that Intelligent and Receptive Power in You
It Will Bring You Comfort and Open Your Eyes

The most important work of our life as Christians is to love God, love others, and to strengthen our faith daily. Faith is never accidental; it is deliberate—and for us, it should be inevitable! You see, faith comes when we hear and develop an implicit trust in God. Do you realize that your faith is actually seeking for its own comfort? Let me give you a hint: **True comfort is found when you are in contact with God.**

Faith has intelligence. It is actually in you by the work of

God and it's very disciplined—but it doesn't stack up and it's nontransferable, so you have to build your own. You see, some people try to live on other people's faith, but God made faith uniquely personal. Until *your* faith is developed that "He is able," you won't receive the best God has for *you*.

The reason why faith is so essential is because of its receptive power. First things first, those two blind men had settled it in their mind that Jesus was the Son of David. In that revelation, they understood the grandeur of His mission. I love that. Let me say it again: Faith has intelligence!

Your FAITH—It Will Make You Eager to Receive
It's Not Just an Emotion; It's a Conviction of Understanding

I want you to see that faith is not merely an emotion; it's a conviction of understanding. That's what made those two men so eager to receive. They couldn't even see, yet they found Jesus in that house.

Is your faith eager to receive? Your eagerness to follow Jesus will develop your faith quicker than you think. It's the beginning of great things to come. Why? Because being eager to follow Jesus means you'll pursue *"hearing, and hearing by the Word of God."*

Faith is always now. *"Now faith is…"* **(Hebrews 11:1). Yet, although it is "now," it also has the power to produce your future.** Every day, you are moving towards something; let your faith move you in the right direction. Aim for the Lord. Aim for His promises.

You are capable of so much and you owe it to yourself to develop that conviction of understanding. Always aim for the best, knowing that your personal best is always going to be found when you eagerly follow after Jesus.

Chapter Nine Faith Declarations

Yes, Lord! I Believe!

My faith is giving me the **power to discover God.**

My faith is giving me the **passion to cry out to Him.**

My faith is giving me the **tenacity to follow-through.**

My faith is giving me the **openness to "hear" His question.**

My faith is giving me the **guts and honesty to assess myself.**

My faith is giving me the **eyes to see the miracle of truth.**

My faith is giving me the **eagerness to hear the Word.**

My faith is giving me the **readiness to receive His best.**

My faith is giving me the **desire for the prayer of agreement.**

My faith is giving me the **attention of God as I join others in prayer.**

Faith Testimony

I would like to thank you and your ministry, and especially our heavenly Father, for the wonderful healing of my older sister from cancer. Thank you for your healing prayers. She is healed completely from cancer. —**Australia**

Chapter Ten

Refuse to Shipwreck Your Own Faith

F aith is an actual "substance" that God put inside of you. It is made of "things you hope for." When you use faith, it actually becomes "evidence" of things you don't see, which means that it is a force within you that draws those things you hope for towards you.

Most importantly, I think, the Bible made sure to let you know that it was only "for by it" that the elders (all born before you) were able to obtain approval from God. Their good report was obtained by passing the faith test.

Hold Onto Your Faith and Good Conscience
Your Future is Being Made Today

When the Apostle Paul was writing to Timothy, his protégé, about how to live the life of Christianity, he said, *"This charge I commit unto thee, son Timothy, according to the prophecies which went before on thee, that thou by them mightest war a good warfare; Holding faith, and a good conscience; which some having put away concerning faith have made shipwreck"* (1 Timothy 1:18-19).

Now, let's stop right there! The Apostle Paul says right here that you can shipwreck your own faith by doing what? By putting it away. I know a lot of people today who are doing exactly what the Apostle Paul told Timothy not to do. Why anyone would ever want to put aside their faith boggles my mind because, as Christians, we know that without faith, it's impossible to please God. Yet, even preachers are doing it.

I know every one of you want to be a success in life—and faith is the key to success. It is very important that we do what Paul said and make "holding faith" and "a good conscience" our priority. The future—who we are going to be and what we are going to do—is being made each and every day.

Let Your Faith Be Your Soul's Eye, Ear, and Hand
Your Faith Can Handle Conflict Well

So, my first point is this: **Faith directs your attention to the resistance of all evil and the cultivation of all good.** That's why the Apostle Paul called it warfare. If you will allow it, your faith can handle conflict very well. Faith is the soul's eye and by it we can see what the natural eye cannot see.

Faith is also the soul's ear. It can hear what the natural ear can't hear. It is also the soul's hand in that it can handle what the natural hand cannot handle. Let me say it again to you, because I really want you to get this: Faith can handle conflict very well. Think about it for a minute.

Faith supplies motives for endurance. It supplies hope for success. The reason faith can supply these things is because it gives you confidence in your leader, Jesus Christ, and in yourself. Glory! Now you can understand why the Word says to live by faith and not by sight—you need faith for a good life.

If Your Faith Decays, There is a Shipwreck in Your Future
Don't Divorce Your Faith from Your Life

Now, my second point is this: **We have a Christian faith to hold onto and a Christian life to lead. You must not look at them apart from each other. Your faith is the support of your life.** You must never divorce your faith from your everyday life. Why? Because if your faith decays, there is a shipwreck in your future.

I create my future every day with my faith—I say what I *want*, not what I *need*. So, from my thoughts to my words to my actions, my focus is going beyond need—I'm directing my attention to the resistance of evil and the cultivation of good.

God's Word is true. The Word says He supplies all our needs according to His riches in glory, so I don't deal with need. Again, God's Word is true! My faith is in Him and you may have heard me say it many times before, "I tell God what I want, not what I need."

Some people like to try and paint that as greed, but I say, "NO! That's growth!" I've already gotten beyond need in my faith-life! I've grown a little bit and I know without a shadow of doubt that ALL my needs will be met in Him—it's a done deal. Next! I'm going higher. I'm moving into my destiny; not towards the desires of *my* heart, but towards the desires of *His* heart. He always takes care of me when I put Him first—that's a promise!

Never Underestimate the Glory of Duty
When Your Faith and Conscience Are at the Same High Level, Manifestation is Automatic

My third point is this: **When your faith and your conscience are on the same high level, manifestation becomes automatic— spiritually, physically, and financially.** That's a huge part of living the Christian life well—holding onto your faith through it all and keeping your conscience fully clean at the same time. Just see what God will do for you and through you for others—it will amaze you.

The way of faith is not the way of man's intellect. It is beyond "reason" and is simply duty. It's your duty to believe what the Word says. Duty will bring you to the feet of God.

Can't you hear Jesus saying, *"Not My will, but Thine, be done"*? Jesus was living by His faith in His Father and keeping a clear conscience, which means He was doing His duty. Look at the results that it got Him: healings, miracles, wisdom, prophecy, power, and manifestation like we've never seen. Christ's faith levels were off the charts, and it showed. His conscience was also cleaner than anyone who lived before or after Him. He was literally the only one who held out and never sinned—why? So He could fulfill His duty, which was the cross.

That cruel cross was Jesus' destiny and duty, and He fulfilled both when His final day on this earth came to pass. Sinless and full of faith, Jesus paid the price and became the ultimate sacrifice for everything mankind lost, lacked, and had done wrong, making a way for each of us to be saved. No matter what we've done, we can accept His sacrifice for us simply by faith, and we get a fresh, clean slate in our life from God as a result. Our good conscience begins the moment we let Him wash our sin away, and it's by faith that we do that.

Never underestimate the glory of doing your duty.

Never Let Go of the Basics
Out of Basic Duties, You Will Rise to Meet Your Destiny

Every single person on this earth has a duty to perform, and whether it's big or small in the eyes of others, doesn't matter at all. What matters is that you do the most basic of your duties by having faith in God and keeping your conscience clean, and you will naturally move towards other duties and opportunities in the life you've been given. Remember to never let go of the basics. Out of the basic duties of faith and a good conscience, you will rise to meet your destiny.

Remember that your faith pleases God, so keep living *"For by it"*—by FAITH!

Chapter Ten Faith Declarations

I refuse to shipwreck my own life!

I'm holding onto my faith!

I'm keeping my conscience clean!

My faith can handle conflict well!

I'm putting God first and He's taking care of me!

I refuse to divorce my faith from my everyday life!

I resist all evil and cultivate all good!

My faith is beyond "reason"—it's my duty!

I will not be shipwrecked!

I'm rising up to meet my destiny!

Faith Testimony

I was told by doctors that I had lymphoma cancer. But I told them from the very beginning, no, I did not have cancer. I prayed about it and my faith never waivered. They wanted to start chemo and I said no. After further testing, they found the cancer was gone. Thank You, Jesus! **—Facebook**

DVD Companion to This Book:

If You Don't Know What IT is, You Won't Get IT

Other Books by Jesse Duplantis:

Why Isn't My Giving Working? The Four Types of Giving

*Distortion: The Vanity of Genetically Altered Christianity

*The Everyday Visionary

Breaking the Power of Natural Law

*What In Hell Do You Want?

*Wanting a God You Can Talk To

*Jambalaya for the Soul

*God Is Not Enough, He's Too Much!

*Heaven: Close Encounters of the God Kind

The Ministry of Cheerfulness

All these titles can be ordered online at www.jdm.org.

*Also available as an eBook.

Prayer of Salvation

Friend, God loves you and desires to give you a new life of real joy and peace. He wants you healed, delivered, prosperous, and set free from anything that is holding you back. For you to experience this new life, all you have to do is accept His divine plan of salvation through His only Son, Jesus Christ.

Jesus Christ paid the price for all your sin with His shed blood on the cross. He died and rose again so that you could spend eternity with Him in Heaven, and live a blessed life here on Earth. If you are ready to make Him your Lord and Savior, simply open your heart to Him and say this prayer…

Jesus, come into my life. Forgive me of my sins. I ask You to cleanse my heart and make me a new person in You right now. I believe that You are the Son of God and that You were sent by the Father to die on the cross for me. Jesus, I want to thank You for loving me enough to die for me. I accept all that Your shed blood bought for me on the cross and I receive You as my Savior and Lord. Amen.

If you just prayed this prayer, congratulations! You are a "new creature" in Christ and, as 2 Corinthians 5:17 says, *"…old things have passed away; behold, all things are become new."* You have a whole new life of faith and victory ahead of you!

It is important that you let someone know of your decision to follow Christ, and we would love to hear from you. You can contact us at:

Jesse Duplantis Ministries
PO Box 1089
Destrehan, LA 70047
985.764.2000
www.jdm.org